Celeste, a worker for a conservation group, is trapped!

Travelling up a jungle river in South America, Celeste is gathering information to help save the environment around the river. Celeste's observations have already revealed how pollution and logging are having a devastating effect on the river and jungle.

Suddenly, halfway through the trip, disaster strikes! Because of their boat's broken propeller, Celeste and her fellow travellers become trapped in the dangerous jungle. Behind them are the rocks of a cave and, in front of them, the snarling, gleaming teeth of a jaguar!

high, screaming sound that tore through the night air."

Chapter 1.

The deadly jaguar crouched low and let out a menacing growl. Its green eyes shone in our torchlight and it drew back its lips. Two curved, yellow fangs gleamed as it growled again. It glared fearlessly at the three people huddled together in the darkness.

"Celeste, stay still. Don't move a muscle!" whispered Miguel in a terrified voice.

I kept my eyes on the dangerous cat. Miguel didn't need to warn me. My whole body was frozen in fear. The jaguar slowly circled around the entrance to the cave where we were sheltering. Its muscles were powerful, and its tail swayed slowly from side to side. We were in trouble. Deep trouble.

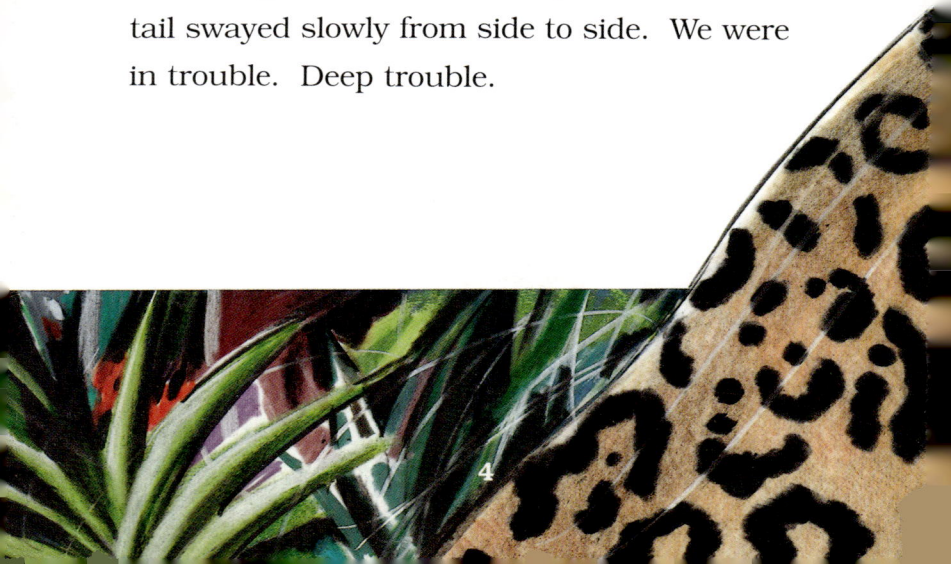

Jaguar Attack!

Written by John Parsons

Illustrated by Donna Cross

Contents	Page

Nelson

an International Thomson Publishing company I(T)P®

Jaguar Attack!

With these characters ...

Celeste

Señor
Paralobo

Miguel And
Felix

The
Timijaro Indians

"It was a

If we were silent and did not move, maybe the jaguar would ignore us. Miguel and I breathed silently and slowly. The slightest noise could cause the jaguar to unleash its deadly attack.

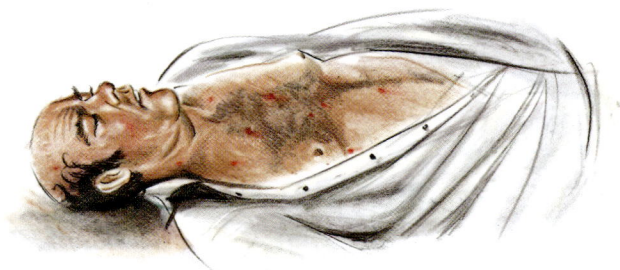

Just then, at the worst possible moment, the figure lying on the ground beside me stirred and shuddered. Señor Paralobo's body was covered in mosquito bites, and he was terribly ill from malaria. After being unconscious for an hour, sweating silently and sinking further and further into a fever, he was now waking. He let out a loud groan and said something in Portuguese. Instantly, the jaguar's ears dropped flat against its head, and it bared its frightening fangs again. It crouched low and its tail started to wave furiously. It was getting ready to strike. Who would it attack first?

The fearsome jaguar's eyes met mine, and we stared at each other.

"What on earth am I doing here?" I asked myself silently.

Up until three weeks ago, I worked in a comfortable office in Washington, surrounded by newspapers, fax machines and computers. I am a conservation worker, and the closest I had come to dangerous animals, deadly diseases, and the dense jungle, had been through reading articles and reports from our other workers around the world. Now I was facing a deadly jaguar in the middle of a South American jungle. Suddenly, I felt a million kilometres from civilisation.

When the manager of our conservation group had come into my office to ask me if I wanted to do some research in South America, I had jumped at the chance. A logging company had been wanting to cut down thousands of trees along the Timijaro River, and my job was to write a report about their impact on life in and around the river. Our reports are presented to the government in an attempt to stop the logging.

As I stared into the eyes of the growling cat, I wondered if anyone would ever find my diary. I had been using it to note down my observations, for my ecological report on how people were destroying the river.

It seemed a silly thought but, if I was going to be attacked by a jaguar, I didn't want my journey to be wasted.

Chapter 2.

Date: Monday, 12th April.
Time: 9.00 p.m.
Location: Quinjaro City.

Observations:

We are at the start of our expedition. Our goal: to map the Timijaro River and to find its source, high in the Maya mountains. There are three of us in the expedition: Felix, the captain of our small boat; Miguel, a guide who has lived with the dangerous and primitive Indians in the area, and who knows how to survive in the jungle; and myself, Celeste. We have enough supplies for a month. The travelling will be tough. The South American jungle through which we must pass is unexplored and we do not know what danger awaits us. But the preparation for this expedition has been an exciting time. All of us who have gathered here in Quinjaro City, where the Timijaro meets the Atlantic Ocean, are keen to explore inland.

Our plan is to travel in Felix's small red boat, the *Bueno Porto*, as far upstream as we can go. When the river becomes too shallow or too difficult for the *Bueno Porto*, we will return. By venturing into places that nobody has explored before, this will be an adventure to remember!

Along the way, I must write notes about the effect that humans are having on this river. Quitos Timber, a logging company, wants the government to allow it to cut down huge areas of jungle. My job is to convince the government that this is not a responsible idea. Already, the activities of people along the river have had a terrible effect on the environment. More logging will be disastrous. We will lose rare species of plants and animals. The river will become polluted and die.

Tonight, we are all on board the *Bueno Porto*. The boat is tied to a small wharf in the estuary of the Timijaro, the area where the river and the sea meet and mix. The water around us is slow-moving and brown.

On the shores of the river, the city of Quinjaro is busy. Houses and factories line the banks of the river. The water is terribly polluted here, with waste and litter from the city slowly moving downstream.

The only plants that we see above the water are dead trees and the mosses and lichens that cover the thick wooden piles of the wharf. Below us, through the murky water, we can barely see the seaweed that shifts with the tide.

As the tide rises and falls, the river also moves. The salty water of the sea mingles with the fresh water of the river.

At high tide, Miguel points out the small, silvery salt-water fish darting and jumping in the estuary. They are hunted by hungry seagulls that screech above the noise of the ships and the activity at the wharves and in the city. Rusting oil drums and grimy plastic containers along the river's edge collect rainwater and provide ideal places for mosquito larvae to hatch. Each evening, the air is full of clouds of mosquitoes, whining and hovering above us. Miguel tells me I must take care not to get bitten, as mosquitoes can transfer serious diseases to humans.

A dredge, a flat-bottomed boat that digs up soil from the riverbed, is anchored next to us. Miguel says the Timijaro is in constant danger of filling up with soil washed down from upstream. The dredge must work all year round to stop the mouth of the river from closing up. If that happened, the city would be in danger of flooding, as the river tried to find a new way to reach the sea.

Tonight, we must rest. Tomorrow, Felix will start to take us on our journey into the unknown.

Chapter 3.

Date: Tuesday, 13th April.
Time: 5.30 a.m.–10.30 a.m.
Location: Outside Quinjaro City.

Observations:

Before sunrise, we are all awake and making last-minute preparations. Felix says that high tide is at 10.00 a.m., and we must be well upstream before the salty water starts to move back into the sea. The outgoing tide, plus the flow of the river, could make our first day's travelling slow if we find ourselves caught in the estuary.

As our small red boat moves by the city, we pass huge concrete and iron pipes at the river's edge. Some pipes carry water and rubbish that is washed off the city streets. Others carry waste from the factories that line the river. The water is oily and dirty, and not much can live in this part of the Timijaro.

On the banks of the river, a few hardy weeds struggle to survive. Seagulls scavenge food scraps and dead fish that float downstream. The water is slow moving. Even if the waste from the city had not poisoned the river, the slow water means there would be little oxygen for fish to breathe through their gills here.

We are glad when we leave the last of Quinjaro behind us and move into open countryside. By 10.30 a.m., we are out of the estuary, and Quinjaro is just a hazy smudge on the horizon.

Date: Tuesday, 13th April.
Time: 5.00 p.m.
Location: 50 km west of Quinjaro City.

Observations:

This afternoon, Felix lowered our anchor in water that is still brown. But, in the ten hours since we left Quinjaro, we have travelled fifty kilometres, and the pollution of the city is far behind us. On both sides of the Timijaro, farmland stretches as far as we can see. Miguel says it was once all jungle. But, sadly, the trees have gone, and so too have the magnificent plants and animals that once lived here.

The farmland near the river is rocky and flat. That tells us that the river floods here and covers the flat farmland. When the floods arrive, they wash away much of the soil and leave only rocks. The soil is carried downstream to the estuary, where it falls to the riverbed until it is dredged away. The floods remove the soil from where it is needed, and dump it where it is not wanted.

The banks of the river are covered in moss and algae, and there are thick weeds below us, growing up from the riverbed.

The weeds choke the other plants that try to grow here, and they slow the river down. This is a sign of another kind of pollution.

Because the soil and all its nutrients are washed away in every flood, Miguel tells us how the farmers have to use huge quantities of fertiliser and chemicals on their land, so that their grass and crops will grow. Every time it rains, some of the fertiliser and chemicals wash down into the river and are used by the greedy weeds. Eventually, so many weeds will grow that the river will become clogged.

I know, from my research, that so many nutrients will wash into the river that even the weeds will not be able to use them all. The build-up of nutrients will slowly poison this stretch of the river, too. It would be like having to eat mountains of unhealthy food ten times a day: very soon, you would start to feel very ill.

Chapter 4.

Date: Thursday, 15th April.
Time: 8.00 p.m.
Location: 150 km west of Quinjaro City.

Observations:

After two days of travelling upstream through farmland, we are almost at the edge of the jungle. But it is an edge that is constantly being eroded away. As more and more humans need more and more food, the jungle is being cut and burnt down to provide more farmland.

In the evening, the sky is dirty and brown from the smoke of distant forest fires. If a logging company cannot cut down the trees and sell the timber, they simply burn the jungle. Then, they can sell the land to farmers. Either way, the rare plants and animals that once lived here vanish. Who knows what we might lose? Perhaps in one of these plants there is a chemical that might help cure cancer or protect us from some other deadly disease.

Unless we preserve the jungle and research the life that is in it, we will never know.

Miguel points to the horizon, where a dark red glow lights up the evening sky.

"Quitos Timber," he says. "Every day, less jungle."

Here and there, a remaining tree's branches reach out over the water. Occasionally, as an insect drops off a leaf, we see a small ripple. Here, the water is less polluted, and more ripples are made by small fish eagerly gulping down the insects that fall from above.

Tonight, our captain, Felix, moors at a small wharf and another passenger joins us. He is a short man in a dirty white suit. Felix tells us his name is Señor Paralobo. He does not say much to Felix, and prefers to sit alone in the front of the boat. When I ask Felix where he is travelling to, he just shrugs his shoulders.

"As long as he pays, I don't care," he replies.

Miguel and I share our food with Señor Paralobo, and he smiles politely at us.

"Abrogado," he says. Thank you. He speaks only Portuguese, so it is hard for me to talk to him.

Date: Sunday, 18th April.
Time: 4.00 p.m.–10.00 p.m.
Location: 250 km west of Quinjaro City.

Observations:

The smell of smoke is still in the air, even though we are two days from our last stop. But, thankfully, the jungle around the river here is thick and lush. The logging company has not yet reached this far upstream. As Miguel points out the rare species of birds resting in the huge rainforest trees, I make notes. This environment must be preserved, and the best way to do that is to tell the world how beautiful and precious it is.

We see toucans, with their fabulously coloured beaks. We see huge, towering trees, higher than most buildings, and tropical plants, their leaves thick and green. Sometimes, we see the most amazing flowers, rising on huge stems from the middle of plants. I draw them as well as I can, and hope that I will be able to identify them later, when I return to Washington.

Beneath us, we occasionally see silvery flashes of light, as a school of fish dashes away from the propeller blades of the *Bueno Porto*.

"Piranha!" hisses Felix. He makes a chattering noise with his teeth. We all know that a school of piranha can devour a large animal, like a cow or a sheep, in minutes, with their ferocious, razor-sharp teeth.

Señor Paralobo continues to sit alone in the front of the boat. When I glance over at him, I notice that he too is making notes. Perhaps he is working for another conservation group? Or maybe he is just a tourist, keeping a diary of his travels? Who knows? When he catches me looking at him, he just smiles at me. He seems harmless enough.

The water around us is now cleaner and flows faster than further downstream. It is also shallower. Felix must concentrate hard as he guides the *Bueno Porto* through the rocks that lie just below the surface.

At night, after Felix lowers our anchor, we relax and listen to the sounds of the jungle: strange birds calling and unseen insects clicking and scratching their noisy songs to each other. Huge swarms of mosquitoes hover around us, whining loudly as they try to squeeze through the fine nets we have draped over our sleeping bags.

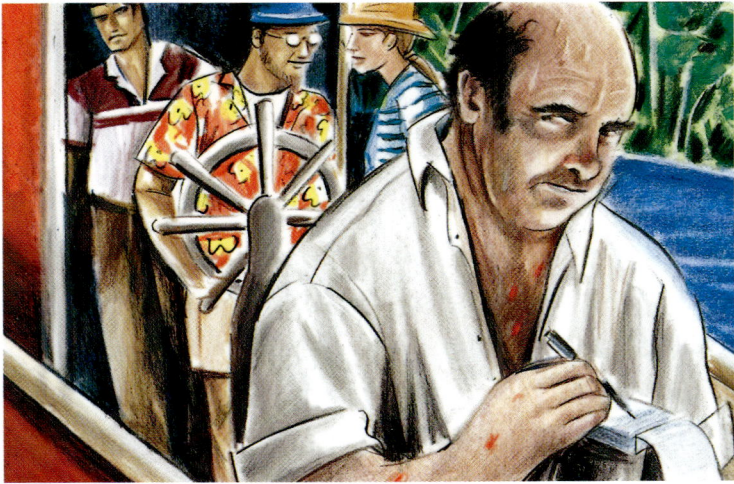

Señor Paralobo remains at the front of the boat, slapping at the mosquitoes that ignore the insect repellent he has smeared all over his face and arms. After an hour, the mosquito attacks drive him into the cabin, where he talks with Felix late into the night.

Chapter 5.

Date: Monday, 19th April.
Time: 11.30 a.m.
Location: 260 km west of Quinjaro City.

Observations:

Today disaster struck! Just after lunch, the *Bueno Porto* hit a rock! Felix immediately reversed the *Bueno Porto*, but the force of the current swept us backwards too rapidly. The boat swung around, and smashed into another rock that was lying just beneath the water's surface. Señor Paralobo was almost thrown into the water by the force of the impact.

Felix instantly dropped our anchor and dived into the river. I hoped there were no piranhas about! He swam underwater, trying to see how bad the damage was. When he clambered back on board the *Bueno Porto*, I could see the news was not good.

"The propeller has broken," he said, dripping water and looking worried.

"We must return downstream," said Miguel. Felix shook his head.

"Sorry, but with no propeller, we are stranded," he said glumly. "If we cannot control the boat, we will smash into every rock along the way. The *Bueno Porto* will be destroyed as the current carries us downstream."

I was alarmed. We were stuck in the middle of the jungle, three days' journey from help. What were we going to do?

Señor Paralobo, Miguel and I looked to Felix for a solution.

"I will paddle the canoe back to our last stop," he said, pointing at the small canoe lashed to the deck of the *Bueno Porto*. "Paddling downstream, it will only take me a day to get back. Then, I will arrange for another boat to pick you up."

We all looked at each other. There was no alternative. The canoe was only big enough for one person.

Date: Wednesday, 21st April.

Time: 8.45 p.m.

Location: 260 km west of Quinjaro City.

Observations:

Felix has been gone for two days, and still there is no sign of rescue. Before he left, he helped us to unload the vital supplies from the *Bueno Porto*. Using the small canoe, we ferried food, medicines, our sleeping bags and mosquito nets over to the nearest shore. There, we would wait.

As Felix paddled off into the distance, a feeling of gloom came over those of us who were left behind. Señor Paralobo sat, resting against a tree, his eyes closed. He looked tired. Miguel and I began to set up a makeshift camp. But soon after, the jungle let us know that our work was wasted. In the distance, a low rumble alerted us to a thunderstorm on its way. We knew that within minutes, our campsite would be flooded with heavy rain. If it rained heavily enough, the river would start to rise and wash away our supplies. We had to shift to higher ground.

"Follow me," said Miguel calmly.

As we climbed up the bank of the river, we pushed our way through thick jungle. A few metres away, the jungle cleared, and Miguel spotted a small, dark cave in the rocky hillside.

"Over there," he said. "We can shelter in the cave until the storm has passed."

We hurried back to the river's edge to gather our supplies. When we arrived, we saw instantly that things were going to become a lot worse.

Señor Paralobo had collapsed against the tree, and was moaning and gasping. He was covered in sweat, and he looked terribly ill. Miguel rushed up to him and loosened his shirt so he could breath more easily. Immediately, we saw what the problem was. Señor Paralobo's neck and chest were covered with mosquito bites.

"Malaria," said Miguel in a worried voice.

We dragged Señor Paralobo up the riverbank to the cave and tried to make him comfortable. I raced back to the river and hunted through my medical supplies. Just then, I noticed a small white card on the ground, where Señor Paralobo had collapsed. I picked it up. With a feeling of intense shock, I read what was on it.

"Señor Jose Paralobo," it said. "Engineer, Quitos Timber Company."

I gasped. I realised that Señor Paralobo was not a conservationist or a tourist at all. He had been investigating the river and the jungle for the logging company. He was the enemy!

Chapter 6.

Although I felt angry towards Señor Paralobo, there was no time to worry about that now. I found the medicine, and carried as many bags of supplies up the bank as I could, just as the heavy rain started to pound down. It was a deluge. I knew then why they called the jungle a 'rainforest'!

As night fell, we sheltered in the cave. We had enough food for another few days, but Señor Paralobo needed to get to a hospital. We were worried. Where was Felix? When would help arrive?

Just as we were starting to think that things could not get any worse, they did. Above the sound of the thunder and the rain came an even more terrifying sound.

It was a high-pitched scream that tore through the night air. It was the sound of a jaguar calling. And it was close. Very close.

The snarl of the jaguar brought me back to the present. My mind had been racing as I remembered the journey that had brought me face to face with the deadly predator. The jaguar's eyes burned into mine as we stared at each other. Señor Paralobo groaned and mumbled words that didn't make any sense. He was shaking with fever, and the sweat poured off his face.

"Don't move," Miguel whispered again. But it was no use. The jaguar tensed its muscles and crouched down low, ready to leap towards us.

Suddenly, something shot through the air past my head. The jaguar let out an angry roar and jumped backwards in alarm. Something else whizzed past my head, and the jaguar snarled in rage.

It twisted its enormously powerful body and leapt away from us. With another snarl, it disappeared instantly into the jungle beyond the clearing.

I turned to see what had frightened off the jaguar and instantly froze again.

In the darkness of the jungle stood a group of shadowy figures.

As they moved silently towards us, I could see that they were human. They were Timijaro Indians—the mysterious, dangerous people of the jungle.

A short time later, in a tiny village deep within the jungle, Señor Paralobo was weakly sipping a mixture of water and tree bark that the Indians had boiled up as a medicine. Miguel listened and translated as the leader of the Indians spoke to us. My eyes were fixed on the leader. He was small, but had strong muscles, just like the jaguar. His body was covered in paint. His dark hair was cut straight across his forehead. His eyes were black, and he looked fearsome. His voice, though, was gentle and soft.

"Tomorrow, he will be well enough to travel. We will take you all back to the edge of the jungle in our canoes. But we will take you no further," translated Miguel.

"I can see you think we are dangerous and primitive. But we understand the jungle better than you, so we can help."

He nodded towards Señor Paralobo.

"We know the plants that give us medicine to fight sickness. All that *you* know is how to burn them."

The Indian leader sighed, and gestured towards the surrounding rainforest.

"We have lived here since the start of time. This is our home, and we treat it with respect. You, who burn our home and destroy our river, think that *we* are dangerous and primitive?"

The man looked straight at me as he spoke, and his eyes looked sad. Not sad for himself, but sad for me! He shook his head.

"It is *you* who are dangerous and primitive," he said. "I only hope you have enough time left to learn how to be civilised."

I nodded. I couldn't wait to return to Washington. Not to get back to my comfortable life in an office, away from jaguars and disease and Indians, but to start one of the most important jobs of my life: the campaign to save what was left of the Timijaro River.

"The river silently glides ..."

Like a slow-moving snake,
The river silently glides
Along its slow, winding course.
The only sound, the hiss of the rain.

Like a caterpillar chewing,
The chain-saws inch forward
To the heart of the jungle.
Along the edge, the sound of destruction.